CAROLINA PANTHERS

BY ALEX MONNIG

The Child's World®

Published by The Child's World®
1980 Lookout Drive • Mankato, MN 56003-1705
800-599-READ • www.childsworld.com

Acknowledgments
The Child's World®: Mary Berendes, Publishing Director
Red Line Editorial: Editorial direction
The Design Lab: Design
Amnet: Production

Design Element: Dean Bertoncelj/Shutterstock Images
Photographs ©: Mike McCarn/AP Images, cover; Brynn
Anderson/AP Images/Corbis, 5, 11; Matt A. Brown/
NewSport/Corbis, 7; Ruth Fremson/AP Images,
9; Shutterstock Images, 13; Margaret Bowles/AP Images,
14-15; Charles Rex Arbogast/AP Images, 17; G. Newman
Lowrance/AP Images, 19; Bob Leverone/AP Images,
21; Morry Gash/AP Images, 23; Jim Dedmon/Icon
Sportswire/Corbis, 25; Cliff Welch/Icon SMI/Corbis, 27;
Chuck Burton/AP Images/Corbis, 29

ISBN 9781634070126
LCCN 2014959717

Printed in the United States of America
Mankato, MN
July, 2015
PA02265

ABOUT THE AUTHOR

Alex Monnig is a freelance journalist from St. Louis, Missouri, who now lives in Sydney, Australia. He has traveled across the world to cover sporting events in China, India, Singapore, New Zealand, and Scotland. No matter where he is, he always makes time to keep up to date with his favorite teams from his hometown.

TABLE OF CONTENTS

GO, PANTHERS!

The Carolina Panthers started playing in 1995. They had some early success. Then the Panthers had some terrible seasons. The team is located in Charlotte, North Carolina. That area has many college basketball fans. But the Panthers have built a big following. The team often has a strong defense that keeps other teams out of the end zone. Let's meet the Panthers.

Panthers quarterback Cam Newton charges forward with the ball against the Atlanta Falcons on December 28, 2014.

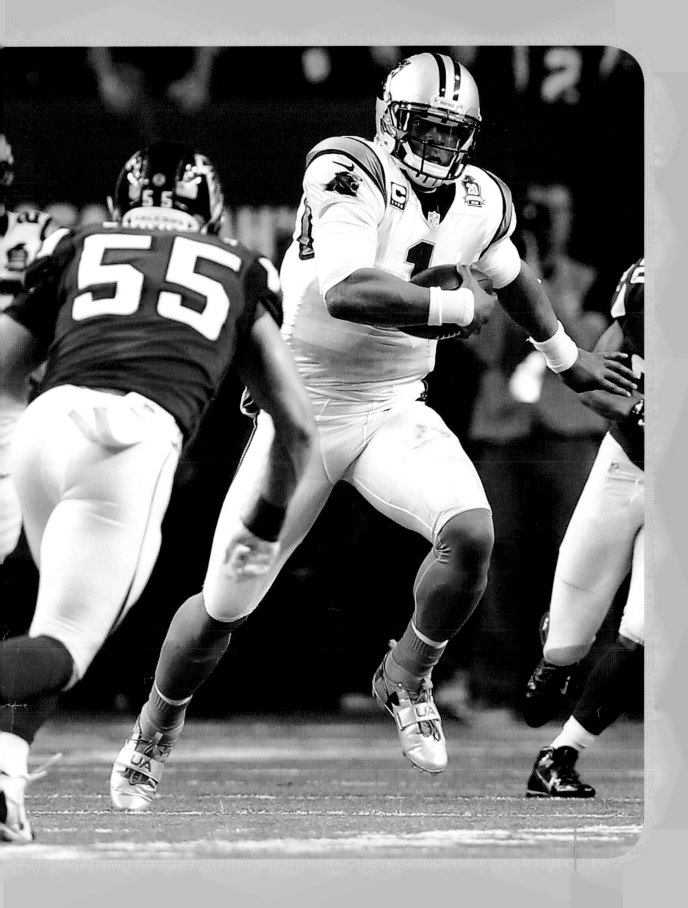

WHO ARE THE PANTHERS?

The Carolina Panthers play in the National Football **League** (NFL). They are one of the 32 teams in the NFL. The NFL includes the American Football Conference (AFC) and the National Football Conference (NFC). The winner of the AFC plays the winner of the NFC in the **Super Bowl**. The Panthers play in the South Division of the NFC. They played in the NFC West before moving to the South. Carolina lost in its only Super Bowl appearance.

Panthers wide receiver Muhsin Muhammad makes an 85-yard catch against the New England Patriots in Super Bowl XXXVIII on February 1, 2004.

WHERE THEY CAME FROM

The NFL wanted to add two teams in 1995. The Panthers were one of them. The Jacksonville Jaguars were the other. Carolina went 7–9 that first season. That was the best record an **expansion** team has ever had in its first season. Things got even better next season. The Panthers made it to the NFC Championship Game. The 2003 Panthers made the Super Bowl. However, they lost to the New England Patriots on a last-minute field goal.

Panthers running back Derrick Moore runs with the ball against the New Orleans Saints on October 22, 1995.

WHO THEY PLAY

The Carolina Panthers play 16 games each season. With so few games, each one is important. Every year, the Panthers play two games against each of the other three teams in their division. They are the Atlanta Falcons, the New Orleans Saints, and the Tampa Bay Buccaneers. The Panthers also play six other teams from the NFC and four from the AFC. The Panthers and Falcons are **rivals**. Atlanta and Charlotte are not far from each other. That means both teams' fans can easily travel to away games.

Panthers linebacker Luke Kuechly (59) tackles Atlanta Falcons wide receiver Julio Jones on December 28, 2014.

WHERE THEY PLAY

The Panthers actually got their start in South Carolina. They played in Memorial Stadium in 1995. That is the home of the Clemson University football team. The Panthers moved into Ericsson Stadium in Charlotte in 1996. It is now called Bank of America Stadium. That is still Carolina's home. It holds 73,778 fans. The Panthers won all nine games in the stadium that first season. That included a playoff win over the Dallas Cowboys.

Bank of America Stadium includes training facilities, practice fields, and team offices for the Panthers.

THE FOOTBALL FIELD

HASH MARKS →

BENCH AREA

GOAL POST →

END ZONE

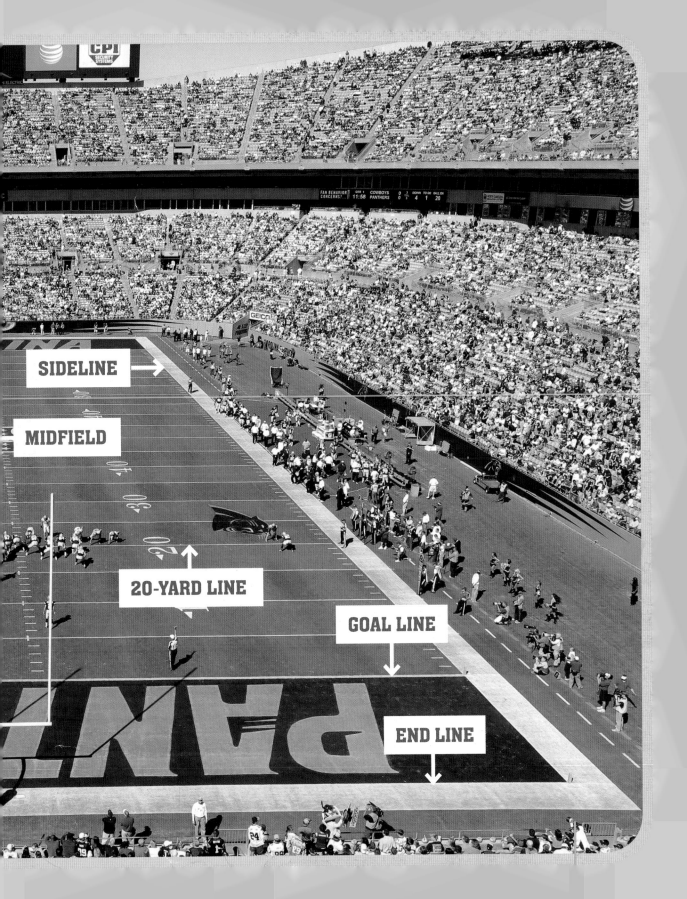

SIDELINE

MIDFIELD

20-YARD LINE

GOAL LINE

END LINE

BIG DAYS

The Panthers have had some great moments in their history. Here are three of the greatest:

1996—Carolina quickly made its presence felt. The Panthers went 12-4. They won the NFC West. Then Carolina got its first playoff win. The Panthers beat the Dallas Cowboys 26-17. Few expected such success from the second-year team.

2004—The 2003 Panthers played the St. Louis Rams in the playoffs on January 10. The Rams scored 11 points in the final 2:44 to tie the game. Neither team scored in the first **overtime**. But Steve Smith scored a touchdown on the first play of double overtime. Carolina moved on and eventually made the Super Bowl.

Panthers wide receiver Steve Smith celebrates after scoring the game-winning touchdown in double overtime against the St. Louis Rams in a playoff game on January 10, 2004.

2009—The Panthers dominated on the ground. Running backs Jonathan Stewart and DeAngelo Williams did most of the work. They became the first teammates to both rush for more than 1,100 yards in the same season.

TOUGH DAYS

Football is a hard game. Even the best teams have rough games and seasons. Here are some of the toughest times in Panthers history:

2001—The Panthers went 1-15. That was the worst record in team history. It was also the worst record in the league. Usually that would mean Carolina had the first pick in the next **NFL Draft**. But Carolina did not even get that. The Houston Texans were entering the league in 2002. So they got the first pick.

2004—The 2003 Panthers made the Super Bowl. They played the New England Patriots on February 1, 2004. Carolina scored with 1:13 left to tie the game. Then came kicker John Kasay's blunder. He sent the kickoff out of bounds. That gave New England good field position. The Patriots kicked the winning field goal with four seconds left.

Panthers quarterback Jake Delhomme is sacked during a September 28, 2009, game against the Dallas Cowboys.

2009—Quarterback Jake Delhomme had had some success. He led the Panthers to the playoffs three times from 2003 to 2008. Carolina signed him to a big **contract** before the 2009 season. But Delhomme fell apart. He was released after the 2009 season.

MEET THE FANS

Carolina Panthers fans love going to games. The team ranks in the top 10 in attendance most seasons. Many of the games sell out. Mascot Sir Purr gets fans going on game days. He has been around since 1995. Carolina fans also love PurrCussion. That is the team's group of 27 drumming performers. They play during breaks in the game.

Panthers quarterback Cam Newton (1) hands a ball to some young fans during a game against the Cleveland Browns on December 21, 2014.

HEROES THEN

Wide receiver Steve Smith was not big. But he was fast and tough. He played for the Panthers from 2001 to 2013. In 2005, he led the NFL with 103 receptions, 1,563 receiving yards, and 12 touchdown catches. Linebacker Jon Beason made the **Pro Bowl** from 2008 to 2010. But defensive end Julius Peppers was Carolina's all-time best defender. He played with the team from 2002 to 2009. He made the Pro Bowl five times during that span. Peppers was the 2002 NFL Defensive **Rookie** of the Year.

Panthers defensive end Julius Peppers battles with a member of the Chicago Bears during a playoff game on January 15, 2006.

HEROES NOW

Quarterback Cam Newton is a dual threat. He has a strong arm. He is also a fast runner. Plus, his large size makes him tough to tackle. Newton was the 2011 NFL Offensive Rookie of the Year. Linebacker Luke Kuechly was great right away. He was the 2012 NFL Defensive Rookie of the Year. Then he was the 2013 NFL Defensive Player of the Year. He proved to be a strong leader even when he was young. Running back Jonathan Stewart has had some injuries. But he has also had some strong rushing seasons.

Panthers linebacker Luke Kuechly prepares to make a play against the Tampa Bay Buccaneers on December 14, 2014.

GEARING UP

NFL players wear team uniforms. They wear helmets and pads to keep them safe. Cleats help them make quick moves and run fast. Some players wear extra gear for protection.

THE FOOTBALL

NFL footballs are made of leather. Under the leather is a lining that fills with air to give the ball its shape. The leather has bumps, or "pebbles." These help players grip the ball. Laces help players control their throws. Footballs are also called "pigskins" because some of the first balls were made from pig bladders. Today, they are made of leather from cows.

Panthers running back DeAngelo Williams runs with the ball against the Tampa Bay Buccaneers on September 7, 2014.

HELMET

SHOULDER PADS

GLOVES

THIGH PADS

KNEE PADS

FOOTBALL

27

SPORTS STATS

Here are some of the all-time career records for the Carolina Panthers. All the stats are through the 2014 season.

PASSING YARDS

Jake Delhomme 19,258

Cam Newton 14,426

RUSHING YARDS

DeAngelo Williams 6,846

Jonathan Stewart 4,825

INTERCEPTIONS

Chris Gamble 27

Eric Davis 25

RECEPTIONS

Steve Smith 836

Muhsin Muhammad 696

SACKS

Julius Peppers 81.0

Charles Johnson 62.5

POINTS

John Kasay 1,482

Steve Smith 454

Panthers wide receiver Steve Smith celebrates after scoring a touchdown against the San Francisco 49ers in a playoff game on January 12, 2014.

TOTAL TOUCHDOWNS

Steve Smith 75

DeAngelo Williams 53

GLOSSARY

contract an agreement about how much and for how long a team pays a player

expansion when a league grows by adding a team or teams

league an organization of sports teams that compete against each other

NFL Draft a meeting of all the NFL teams at which they choose college players to join them

overtime extra time that is played when teams are tied at the end of four quarters

Pro Bowl the NFL's all-star game, in which the best players in the league compete

rivals teams whose games bring out the greatest emotion between the players and the fans on both sides

rookie a player playing in his first season

Super Bowl the championship game of the NFL, played between the winners of the AFC and the NFC

FIND OUT MORE

IN THE LIBRARY

Editors of Sports Illustrated Kids. *Sports Illustrated Kids Big Book of Who: Football.* New York: Time Home Entertainment, 2013.

Fowler, Scott. *100 Things Panthers Fans Should Know & Do Before They Die.* Chicago: Triumph Books, 2013.

Frisch, Nate. *Carolina Panthers.* Mankato, MN: Creative Education, 2013.

ON THE WEB

Visit our Web site for links about the Carolina Panthers:
childsworld.com/links

Note to Parents, Teachers, and Librarians: We routinely verify our Web links to make sure they are safe and active sites. So encourage your readers to check them out!

INDEX